M000206390

LAWLESS LABS

LAWLESS LABS
GOOD LABS GONE BAD

Text by Karin Ronnow

WILLOW CREEK PRESS

For Sammy and Clyde, Labs who left indelible pawprints.

Published by Willow Creek Press
P.O. Box 147, Minocqua, Wisconsin 54548

Photo Credits: p.2 © Biosphoto/Decante Frédéric/Peter Arnold, Inc.; p.6 © C Steimer/Peter Arnold Inc.; p.9 © Denver Bryan/Kimballstock.com; p.10 © Johnny Johnson/AnimalsAnimals; p.13 © C Steimer/Peter Arnold Inc.; p.14 © Denver Bryan/Kimballstock.com; p.17 © age fotostock/SuperStock; p.18 © Denver Bryan/Kimballstock.com; p.21 © Barbara Reed/AnimalsAnimals; p. 22 © Bob Shirtz/SuperStock; p.25 © Maryellen Silliker/AnimalsAnimals; p.26 © Michael Habicht/AnimalsAnimals; p.29 © OSF/Benvie Niall/AnimalsAnimals; p.30 © Ron Kimball/Kimballstock.com; p.33 © C Steimer/Peter Arnold Inc.; p.34 © Jean Michel Labat/ardea.com; p.37 © WILDLIFE/Peter Arnold Inc.; p.38 © Denver Bryan/Kimballstock.com; p.41 © Jerry Shulman/SuperStock; p.42 © Johnny Johnson/AnimalsAnimals; p.45 © Renee Stockdale/Kimballstock.com; p.46 © Denver Bryan/Kimballstock.com; p.49 © Denver Bryan/Kimballstock.com; p.50 © C.C. Lockwood/AnimalsAnimals; p.53 © Chris Harvey/ardea.com; p.54 © Tré Taylor/Images on the Wildside; p.57 © Jean Michel Labat/ardea.com; p.58 © Denver Bryan/Images on the Wildside; p.61 © Sydney Thomson/AnimalsAnimals; p.62 © C Steimer/Peter Arnold Inc.; p.65 © C Steimer/Peter Arnold Inc.; p.66 © Tré Taylor/Images on the Wildside; p.69 © Jean Michel Labat/ardea.com; p.70 © age fotostock/SuperStock; p.73 © Tré Taylor/Images on the Wildside; p.74 © John Daniels/ardea.com; p.77 © Close Encounters of the Furry Kind/Kimballstock.com; p.78 © John Daniels/ardea.com; p.81 © Eunice Pearcy/AnimalsAnimals; p.82 © Johan de Meester/ardea.com; p.85 © Tré Taylor/Images on the Wildside; p.86 © Jean Michel Labat/ardea.com; p.89 © Johnny Johnson/AnimalsAnimals; p.90 © Ron Kimball/Kimballstock.com; p.93 © Johnny Johnson/AnimalsAnimals; p.94 © Lucidio Studio Inc/SuperStock

Editor: Andrea Donner
Printed in Canada

LAB LOVERS BEWARE:

These dogs are not necessarily as adorable and sweet as they appear to be. This book, by way of example and in the spirit of public service, illustrates the nefarious characteristics typically displayed by this peculiar breed. Obtained from canine crime records throughout the land, the following reports represent a laundry list ranging from serious felonies to minor misdemeanors. Be on the lookout for such suspicious Lab behavior in and around your residence.

NAME: BUTTERSCOTCH, AKA SCOTCH

COLOR: YELLOW

AGE: 9

CHARGE: ATTEMPTED THEFT

Class I Misdemeanor

During a party, Scotch raided a pile of guests' shoes by the door and absconded with an odoriferous boot. Caught in the act, the adult male Lab ignored repeated commands to drop the item. In defiance, he dodged all coordinated attempts by guests to retrieve the shoe. Precisely when those attempts were abandoned, Scotch extracted its liner and surrendered the shoe, largely undamaged. Typically a lesser offense, the caper was filed as a Class I misdemeanor due to Scotch's record of recidivism regarding footwear.

NAME: KERMIT
COLOR: BLACK
AGE: Old enough to know better

CHARGE: RECKLESS EXUBERANCE
Class IV Misdemeanor

Kermit retrieved a long branch and proceeded to run around, whacking everything in his way. His reckless gallivanting was deemed a danger to others after he knocked over a small child, and a danger to himself when, in his high-speed attempt to flee the scene, Kermit dashed into a gap between two trees narrower than the stick he carried. The charges were dropped after authorities noted that the child was uninjured and Kermit's contrite owner's admission that, "That dog gets crazy as a bag of ferrets after a front moves through."

NAME: BARNEY
COLOR: CHOCOLATE
AGE: 4

CHARGE: PUBLIC NUISANCE
Class I Misdemeanor

On a snowy February morning, Barney was seen criss-crossing a frozen lake without permission. The normally well-behaved Lab refused to wait for his owner and took off across the lake, breaking trail in every direction. Cross-country skiers and snowmobilers seeking to enjoy the winter wonderland were peevish as they attempted to follow trails that led only in circles. The charges were reduced, and then dropped against the affable Barney when the aggrieved parties declined to sign the complaint.

NAME: FERGIE
COLOR: YELLOW
AGE: 10 WEEKS

CHARGE: BREAKING AND ENTERING
Class II Misdemeanor

A juvenile yellow Lab, Fergie, reported missing at a family reunion picnic, was discovered emerging from a picnic basket containing eight pesto-chicken sandwiches. Authorities considered Fergie's bloated belly the smoking gun in the case. Since food was abundant at the function and it was a first offense, the charges were suspended pending no further similar behavior, or when Fergie reaches adulthood, at which time they'll be expunged from the record. Fergie slept through the legal proceedings.

NAMES: BONNIE AND CLYDE
COLOR: BLACK AND CHOCOLATE
AGES: 4 AND 3

CHARGE: PUBLIC DISRUPTION
Class II Felony

According to witnesses, Bonnie and Clyde raided the city tennis courts, stealing tennis balls and disrupting a high school tennis tournament. Tournament officials allege that as they approached, said dogs fled to the parking lot, leapt into the back of a black pickup truck, and wriggled through an open window into the cab. When questioned by Animal Control officers, the pair denied any connection to the incident. A single tennis ball consistent with the type used at the tournament was discovered in the back of the truck. DNA evidence from the ball proved inconclusive and the pair remains at large.

NAME: DAISY
COLOR: YELLOW
AGE: 3 MONTHS

CHARGE: SOLICITATION
CLASS III Felony (Juvenile)

Apparently upset by what she perceived to be neglect on the part of her owners—who had explained the impractical nature of her demands for 'round-the-clock companionship—Daisy sought comfort from fellow canines in the neighborhood. She was caught leaving the scene of a green doghouse where male Lab puppies are known to congregate. Daisy was sentenced to doggy day care for three months.

NAME: FLETCHER
COLOR: YELLOW
AGE: 5

CHARGE: MUTINY
Class I Felony

After a particularly slow morning of duck hunting on a
Minnesota lake, and while his human companion stood on
the dock, Fletcher organized his crew of decoys, took
control of the boat and floated away. His rebellious
behavior has made him a folk hero among Minnesota's
duck-hunting Labs, but some duck hunters consider him a
criminal. The hunting spot Fletcher selected yielded a
limit, and the charges were dropped with the last duck.

NAME: CAPONE
COLOR: BLACK
AGE: 7

CHARGE: ORGANIZED CRIME, U.S. RICO STATUTES

Class I Felony

According to a federal indictment, since an early age Capone has organized and led gangs of Labs that have established "a pattern of intimidation, extortion, and misappropriation" of a wide range of food and dog toys. Though the gang is not linked to any violence, numerous unexplained litters within the gang's turf are believed traceable to Capone's gang. Authorities took him and his gang of "unedited co-conspirators" into custody following a raid on a local bakery.

NAME: GAWAIN
COLOR: CHOCOLATE
AGE: 1

CHARGE: PERJURY
Class II felony

Caught in the act of pilfering roast beef from a cold-cut tray at a wedding shower, Gawain feigned innocence throughout his trial. In the face of all incriminating evidence and testimony, Gawain appealed to the jury with facial expressions that suggested the evidence and testimony could not possibly apply to him. The jury bought it and Gawain walked. Disappointed prosecutors want to retry him for perjury.

NAME: DINGLE
COLOR: BLACK
AGE: 3

CHARGE: TAMPERING WITH EVIDENCE
Class II Felony

During the winter, Dingle has free reign of the beach, with no sunbathers, swimmers or lifeguards in his way. So come summer, he antagonizes those who invade his turf by raiding their beach bags and burying pilfered items in the sand. It's further alleged that Dingle's MO includes lifting his leg on the beach chairs of his victims. After authorities caught Dingle burying a pair of flip-flops, they dug up his stash and discovered a treasure trove of missing beach items. Dingle was sentenced to his fenced yard for the summer.

NAME: TAYLOR
COLOR: YELLOW
AGE: 4

CHARGE: INDECENT EXPOSURE

Class I Misdemeanor

Taylor's propensity for rolling on her back in the grass, wiggling extensively and exposing herself, riles the elderly couple who lives next door. Local animal behavior authorities suggested to the couple that a male Lab might temper Taylor's promiscuity. The outcome was the opposite, and after living behind closed curtains, the couple and their male Lab moved across town. Shortly thereafter, the statute of limitations ran out on the charges against Taylor.

NAME: HENRY
COLOR: BLACK
AGE: 8

CHARGE: FRATERNIZING WITH THE COMPETITION

Class III Misdemeanor

Henry is a black Lab who knows no boundaries when it comes to making friends. Most recently, however, he has reportedly taken up with a West Highland white terrier, ignoring other Labradors when they come around to play. More egregiously, Henry has adopted some of the Westie's habits, including yipping and nipping. Charges are pending.

NAME: GIBSON
COLOR: YELLOW
AGE: 2

CHARGE: CONDUCT UNBECOMING A LAB

Classless I Misdemeanor

Before he was even a year old, Gibson had a rap sheet for his garden-related crimes, including digging up tulips and other flower bulbs and shredding copies of "Martha Stewart Living" magazine. But after a winter spent indoors watching Martha Stewart on TV, he has adopted peculiar tendencies that include prancing on his hind legs and pointing at various garden plants. Noting Gibson's well-tended hair, the court dismissed the charges, but warned the owner to prohibit Gibson's access to any online stock-trading accounts.

NAME: RUBY
COLOR: YELLOW
AGE: 3 MONTHS

CRIME: BURGLARY
Class II Felony

When pieces of her jewelry began disappearing, Ruby's owner credited the events to her own absentmindedness. But when a pearl necklace she had inherited from her great aunt disappeared, she called the authorities. Police searched the house, and found a cache of jewelry—including the pearl necklace, along with a half-dozen unmatched earrings, two silver bracelets and a class ring—stashed between the couch cushions. Although wholly circumstantial, the evidence landed Ruby in obedience training.

NAME: CASH
COLOR: BLACK
AGE: 1

CHARGE: VOYEURISM
Class II Felony

From the day Cash was tall enough to look over the fence, he began spying on the neighbors. While the situation appeared harmless at first, things became serious when the neighbor's female Lab went into heat and Cash began spending all of his time ogling her. Fearing the worst, the neighbors reported Cash to authorities. Because Cash remained in his own yard while ogling, the charges didn't stick. Cash was nevertheless neutered, which reportedly failed to curb his interest in the neighbor's dog.

NAME: ECHO
COLOR: YELLOW
AGE: 2 MONTHS

CRIME: ECO-TERRORISM
Class III Felony

Shortly after developers of a new subdivision hired landscapers to plant oak saplings, three of the young trees were found dug up. The developers suggested anti-development forces bore responsibility, but when authorities examined the evidence, they found small, sharp teeth marks on the saplings. During a neighborhood stakeout, officers spotted Echo running as fast as her little puppy legs could carry her with a small oak branch in her mouth. Echo was sentenced to her fenced yard unless accompanied by her owner.

NAME: DANDY
COLOR: BLACK
AGE: 8 MONTHS

CHARGE: SERIAL RASCALITY, ELUDING ARREST

Class I Misdemeanor (Juvenile)

Dandy went on the lam after a crime spree that started with chasing deer escalated to chasing livestock, and culminated in snatching and devouring an entire pan of freshly baked brownies from the kitchen counter. Having heard the words, "Bad girl!" too many times, she retreated to her favorite refuge, her owner's duck blind, where she was taken into custody without resistance. The caper landed her in obedience training for eight weeks.

NAME: BAILEY
COLOR: YELLOW
AGE: 7

CHARGE: SHOPLIFTING
Class I Misdemeanor

A pet-store owner reported a large yellow Lab skulking around, and expressed concern that the dog was "casing the store." Police agreed to watch the premises. Two days later, while the storeowner accepted a delivery in the rear of the store, law enforcement observed Bailey's accomplice watch the door while Bailey entered the store and made off with a red dog toy. She was apprehended, toy in mouth, as she came out the door. Inexplicably, the officers paid for the toy and took the pair to the homes listed on their collars. No incident report was filed.

NAME: FINN
COLOR: BLACK
AGE: 4

CHARGE: ROBBERY
Class I Misdemeanor

At a mid-winter Frisbee tournament near his home, Finn, with a proprietary attitude regarding airborne toys, joined in as an unregistered competitor. Finn wasted no time getting between the registered competitors and their owners, expertly intercepting airborne Frisbees of every color and caching them in the woods. With Finn's owner nowhere in sight, the dog catcher was alerted but Finn avoided capture. His large cache of Frisbees was located and the competition resumed. Finn remains at large.

NAME: POGO
COLOR: YELLOW
AGE: 5

CHARGE: TRASH RAID; REPEAT OFFENDER
Class III Felony

When delectable chicken bones were dumped in the trash can, it did not escape Pogo's keen attention. The experienced Lab did not go on full alert, knowing the container was seldom left unattended until emptied. However, when the family left the house, having forgotten about the trash, Pogo struck. Horrified by her owners' quick return, Pogo considered a range of dodges and went with false remorse. The ruse garnered unflattering epithets as Pogo sought refuge behind the couch, where he secretly concluded that it had been well worth it.

NAME: TUCKER
COLOR: BLACK
AGE: 3

CHARGE: PETTY LARCENY
Class I Misdemeanor

A woman called from a California orphanage to report that a large, friendly Labrador had been observed loitering near a Christmas party, but overstayed his welcome when he started looting Santa's gift bag for stuffed animals. The suspect, Tucker, offered no resistance to the dog catcher other than refusing to surrender a Mr. Bill Santa. Tucker was bailed out of the pound after the holiday weekend and sentenced to three days of time served.

NAME: PADDINGTON
COLOR: CHOCOLATE
AGE: 2

CHARGE: LEWD BEHAVIOR; RESISTING ARREST

Class I Misdemeanor

Paddington is well known for his randy ways with neighborhood females, irrespective of their breed. But he pushed it too far when he coupled with an underage Shitzu on its owner's front lawn. When authorities arrived on the scene, Paddington sensed an opportunity for a game of catch-me-if-you-can. He was eventually nabbed and jailed. Paddington was sentenced to his yard and probation.

NAME: POPEYE
COLOR: BLACK
AGE: 8

CHARGE: IMPERSONATING EMERGENCY PERSONNEL (LIFEGUARD)

Class II Felony

Years spent lakeside have led Popeye to claim the beach as his turf. He keeps it scrupulously clear of dead fish and other canines. Evidently believing himself capable of rescue procedures, Popeye periodically accosts sunbathers he believes in need of CPR, and smothers them with kisses. Some find Popeye's concern and affection terrifying and have asked that he be restrained. Lake authorities are prepared to take the matter up in the fall, if Popeye's activities continue until then.

NAMES: TRACE; TRAPPER
COLOR: YELLOW
AGES: 4, 5

CHARGE: 10 COUNTS (AT LEAST) ATTEMPTED HOMICIDE

Crime: Class I Felony

Two yellow Labs who have free reign of a backyard pool have been spotted trying to drown each other. The Lab's owners reported that the activity started as a game, but had advanced to a point where they became concerned and, to teach the dogs a lesson, reported them to authorities. The Labs were banned from the pool for the summer and the owners got a ticket for misuse of emergency 911 communication services.

NAME: BRUNSWICK
COLOR: CHOCOLATE
AGE: 2

CHARGE: GLUTTONY
Class III Misdemeanor

Neighbors who agreed to keep an eye on 2-year-old Brunswick became concerned when they hadn't seen the dog in the yard for several hours. A check by authorities at Brunswick's residence found the dog consuming a gigantic bag of kibbles. The affidavit of probable cause cited the torn kibble bag, Brunswick's inability or unwillingness to stand, and his distended stomach as proof of "gross violation" of house rules. Brunswick's owners declined to press charges.

NAME: TAI
COLOR: YELLOW
AGES: 3 MONTHS

CHARGE: FAILURE TO YIELD

Class I Misdemeanor

Tai, a young yellow Lab (left), has become convinced that every stick, ball, Frisbee or retrieving dummy belongs to him. His belligerence and refusal to share violates the rules of the community dog park, from which he has been banned until he finishes teething.

NAME: DERBY
COLOR: CHOCOLATE
AGE: 9

CHARGE: VAGRANCY; TRESPASSING
Class II Misdemeanors

The owner of a home on the tony end of town reported that a strange Lab had climbed the steps onto her porch, found a place in the sun, reclined and refused to move. Investigators moved Derby to the sun-bathed steps of City Hall and returned him to his owner after work. The complainant reports that her repeated attempts to learn disposition of the case have been "stonewalled" by authorities.

NAME: GUIDO
COLOR: YELLOW
AGE: 6 YEARS

CHARGE: COERCION (UNRELENTING)
Class III Misdemeanor

Although he appears innocent, this beach-dwelling adult male Lab exhibits an inordinate ability to make people act against their will, particularly in regard to throwing a ball. Those who throw the ball for Guido typically do so willingly until they tire and firmly say, "No more." But Guido refuses to relent, using his eyes, a slightly tilted head, and persistence to coerce the victim to continue—often until Guido loses the ball or the sun sets. Because Guido is popular among beachgoers he has yet to victimize, officials are proceeding carefully.

NAME: GOMER
COLOR: YELLOW
AGE: 3 YEARS

CHARGE: GRAND LARCENY (VEHICLE)
Class II Felony

Usually restricted to riding in the bed of his owner's red pickup, Gomer crawled through the truck's rear window, in the process putting the truck in neutral. The vehicle rolled for a distance down a slight incline and came to a stop without further incident. A non-jury trial found that the case did not meet Grand Larceny standards and Gomer walked.

NAME: MACBETH
COLOR: BLACK
AGE: 7

CHARGE: EPISODIC TYRANNY
Class III Felony

Macbeth believes in monarchy, the vesting of supreme power in a single animal—him. Mistaking his AKC papers for a writ of peerage, Macbeth is a self-anointed heir apparent to all things play and food. Most of the time, his demonstrations of entitlement are innocuous. But when things don't go his way, he behaves like a despot or a tyrant. A fragile modus vivendi between Macbeth and his owners has temporarily stayed legal proceedings.

NAME: SAM
COLOR: CHOCOLATE
AGE: 7

CHARGE: BREAKING AND ENTERING
Class I Misdemeanor

The owner of a backcountry cabin reported that, upon opening the dwelling for the season, it appeared that a mature Lab had taken up residence. When officers arrived to investigate, the Lab challenged them at the door, growled once and then the door slammed. The dwelling owner then arrived on the scene and informed investigators that he had adopted the dog and named him Sam. Charges were dismissed.

NAME: TILLY
COLOR: YELLOW
AGE: 7

CHARGE: UNLAWFUL IMPRISONMENT
Class I Felony

Tilly has ruled the roost since she was a puppy. When a kitten was added to the household, Tilly was perturbed, to say the least. To assert her authority, Tilly has taken to trapping the kitty with her body, refusing to let her roam at will. Arbitration resulted in suspended charges for three months to allow the cat time to learn to use its claws.

NAME: COL. MUSTARD
COLOR: YELLOW
AGE: 8 WEEKS

CHARGE: BULLYING
Class III Felon (Juvenile)

From the day he was born, Col. Mustard has, according to court records, "established a pattern of belligerence toward and intimidation of his littermates for the purpose for his own gain." With a mere glance, Col. Mustard is alleged to get them to do whatever he wants—from surrendering their kibble to aiding his multiple escapes from the kennel. Juvenile authorities hammered out a plea arrangement whereby the pup be neutered in lieu of charges.

NAME: FREUD
COLOR: CHOCOLATE
AGE: 3

CHARGE: GOOFINESS
Class III Misdemeanor

Freud likes frogs. When the young owner of this stuffed green frog reported it missing, toy-enforcement author-ities immediately suspected the canine. A high-speed chase through the residence ended when Freud holed up under the bed covers. Freud was cited for speeding and ordered to have his nails trimmed.

NAME: ZULU
COLOR: YELLOW
AGE: 10 WEEKS

CHARGE: TRESPASSING (JUVENILE)
Class I Misdemeanor

Zulu is an unparalleled escape artist who somehow manages to wiggle under the wooden fence around his suburban yard. When loose in the neighborhood, Zulu refuses to come when he is called. His favorite refuge is the neighbor's bushes. The neighbor, who worries about her flower beds, grew weary of the trespassing canine and called the dogcatcher, who scolded Zulu, returned him to his yard and closed the case.

NAME: GATSBY
COLOR: BLACK (middle)
AGE: 8 WEEKS

CHARGE: KIBBLE HOGGING
Class I Misdemeanor (Juvenile)

Gatsby demonstrated attitude and appetite at a young age by dominating the kibble bowl in the puppy pen. He thought he looked like the other pups in the litter, and would be able to get away with his bogarting by simply blending in. A lineup proved otherwise and Gatsby was quickly fingered. He was lead away on a pink leash.

NAME: BACCHUS
COLOR: YELLOW
AGE: 4 MONTHS

CHARGE: MINOR IN POSSESSION OF ALCOHOL (FIRST OFFENSE)

Class II Misdemeanor

During a recent party at a local fraternity, Bacchus, who lives nearby, started lapping at the contents of a punchbowl. Partygoers thought it was amusing and encouraged Bacchus' behavior. Soon, however, Bacchus was teetering around the frat house before passing out on an hors d'oeuvres tray. The pup was allowed to sleep off the charge.

NAME: GUS
COLOR: BLACK
AGES: 2

CHARGE: ASSAULT
Class II Felony

Gus does what is necessary to secure the perimeter of his lakeside home. He took his guard duties too far one day when he dove into the lake to ward off an approaching canoe, grabbed the gunnels, and dumped the canoeists into the lake. Charges were filed by a sheriff's deputy, who was in the bow of the canoe. The rambunctious Lab narrowly escaped prosecution when the deputy dropped the charges because his boss was up for re-election.

NAME: DYLAN
COLOR: YELLOW
AGE: 4

CHARGE: OBSTRUCTING PUBLIC EMPLOYEES
Class III Misdemeanor

City employees called the dog catcher after Dylan, who had escaped from his yard, repeatedly interfered with their attempts to water park lawns on hot summer days. The employees tried to run the dog off by directly targeting him with water. Dylan thought it was a great game, running from hose to hose, barking at the water and leaping into the air to catch the spray. He was captured when he paused to roll in the grass.

NAME: GUTHRIE
COLOR: CHOCOLATE
AGE: 4

CHARGE: PUBLIC BELLIGERENCE

Class III Misdemeanor

Suspected of being a local gang member, an unidentified Lab commandeered a bench in the city park every week-day between 1:30PM and 3PM. He refused to move for the elderly, who previously had used the bench to rest during daily strolls. Several complainants reported that the dog was not aggressive, but weighed too much to be nudged out of the way. A stakeout disclosed that the dog regularly yielded the bench at 3PM and accompanied his owners home from the elementary school across from the park. The charges were dismissed.

NAME: BOJANGLES
COLOR: YELLOW
AGE: 3 MONTHS

CHARGE: MALICIOUS MISCHIEF
Class III misdemeanor

A backyard wedding turned out to be a playground for this yellow Lab pup, who delighted in tearing flower garlands off the picket fence, popping balloons with her sharp puppy teeth, and stealing shrimp off the buffet table. The last straw, however, was her attempt to get the attention of the bride's mother by pulling at her skirt. Bojangles was kenneled for the entire reception and banned from all outdoor parties until she was old enough to demonstrate more self restraint.

NAME: BORIS
COLOR: CHOCOLATE
AGE: 3

CHARGE: INCESSANT BARKING

Class II Misdemeanor

Boris watched the female Lab across the street for months. The two are friendly, but not intimate. When the female went into heat, the male offender, Boris, began spending all his time outside pacing behind his fence, howling, whining and panting. The female appeared oblivious to his remonstrations, which allegedly made Boris howl longer and louder. The neighbors turned him in. Boris was sentenced to remain indoors for ten days.

NAME: CROCKETT
COLOR: YELLOW
AGE: 2 MONTHS

CHARGE: DISTURBING THE PEACE

Class I Misdemeanor

The dog park wasn't the same after Crockett came along. The young dog was thrilled to find a pack of adult Labs to whom he proved to be an annoyance. The alpha male set about putting Crockett in his place, alerting the authorities to his disruptive behavior by growling his displeasure. Crockett and his case were bound over to a park frequented by younger dogs.

NAME: BUSTER
COLOR: CHOCOLATE
AGE: 3

CHARGE: PETTY THEFT
Class III Felony

Evidence of blueberry pie is hard to hide, as Buster discovered. On probation for a previous pie theft conviction, Buster was caught trying to bury a pie tin in the snow. With only one conviction for food theft, Buster is nevertheless alleged to be a career food thief specializing in pies, cakes, and cookies. Buster ducked the current charges when he substituted a purple Frisbee for the pie tin, which has not been found.

NAME: FIGARO
COLOR: YELLOW
AGE: 4

CHARGE: APATHY

Class III Misdemeanor

In the middle of a game of Frisbee, Figaro collapsed on the grass, drank an entire bowl of water, and started panting. He first refused to get back into the game; he then refused to "load up" into his owner's vehicle. His behavior violated the "a tired dog is a good dog" rule and he was promptly replaced in the Frisbee game by his rival, "Sugar."

CASE CLOSED